Growth Hacking Your Life
Practical Tips for Maximum Impact

Godfrey Richard Jackson

Table of Contents

1. Introduction 2
2. Understanding the Growth Hacking Mindset 3
   - 2.1. Sub Chapter Heading: The Importance of Developing a Growth Hacking Mindset 3
   - 2.2. Sub Chapter Heading: Recognizing Growth Opportunities 3
   - 2.3. Sub Chapter Heading: Embracing Failure as Part of the Process 4
   - 2.4. Sub Chapter Heading: Adopting a Data-Driven Approach 4
   - 2.5. Sub Chapter Heading: Constant Experimentation and Iteration 5
   - 2.6. Sub Chapter Heading: Cultivating Agility 5
   - 2.7. Sub Chapter Heading: Harnessing the Power of Collaboration 5
3. Setting the Stage: Defining Your Goals 7
   - 3.1. The Importance of Goals 7
   - 3.2. Setting S.M.A.R.T Goals 7
   - 3.3. The Power of Visualization 8
   - 3.4. Creating A Goal Map 9
   - 3.5. In Conclusion 9
4. Mental Strategies for Persistent Progress 10
   - 4.1. Cultivating a Growth Mindset 10
   - 4.2. The Power of Visualization 10
   - 4.3. Resilience: Bouncing Back from Adversity 11
   - 4.4. Mindfulness and Focus 11
   - 4.5. Embracing an Iterative Mindset 12
5. Healthy Habits: The Foundation of Personal Growth 13
   - 5.1. The Catalysts of Health 13
     - 5.1.1. Physical Wellness 13

- 5.1.2. Mental Well-being ... 14
- 5.1.3. Proper Nutrition ... 14
- 5.2. Embodying Healthy Habits ... 14
  - 5.2.1. Habit Stacking ... 14
  - 5.2.2. Progress Over Perfection ... 15
  - 5.2.3. Accountability ... 15
- 5.3. The Ripple Effect ... 15
- 6. Career Advancement Techniques: Hack Your Way Up ... 16
  - 6.1. Encouraging a Growth Mindset ... 16
  - 6.2. Mastering Your Current Role ... 16
  - 6.3. Building Influential Relationships ... 17
  - 6.4. Branding Yourself ... 17
  - 6.5. Priority on Skill Building ... 18
  - 6.6. Seeking Out and Responding to Feedback ... 18
  - 6.7. Be Adaptable ... 18
- 7. Improving Relationships: Connect Deeper, Grow Together ... 20
  - 7.1. Emotional Intelligence: The Cornerstone ... 20
  - 7.2. Impactful Communication: The Lifeline of Relationships ... 21
  - 7.3. Mutual Respect: The Pillar of Longevity ... 21
  - 7.4. Patience, Understanding, and Empathy: The Essential Triumvirate ... 22
  - 7.5. Building Bonds: Nurture to Flourish ... 22
- 8. Mastering Time Management: More Life in Your Day ... 24
  - 8.1. Understanding Time: The Commodity You Can't Store ... 24
  - 8.2. Keys of Time Management ... 25
  - 8.3. Time Management Techniques ... 25
  - 8.4. Time Management Tools ... 26
  - 8.5. The Outcome of Effective Time Management ... 26
  - 8.6. Reassessing and Refining Your Time Management Strategy ... 27
- 9. Continuous Learning: The Key to Unlimited Growth ... 28

- 9.1. Embracing the Learning Mindset 28
- 9.2. Learning Modalities: Discover the Way That Fits You 29
- 9.3. Find Your Learning Sources 29
- 9.4. Building Consistent Learning Routines 30
- 9.5. Curating and Implementing the Learned Knowledge 30
- 10. Maintaining Balance: Managing Growth Without Burnout 32
  - 10.1. Understanding the Importance of Balance 32
  - 10.2. Recognizing the Symptoms of Burnout 32
  - 10.3. Building Balance into Your Growth Plan 33
  - 10.4. Mastering the Art of Stress Management 34
  - 10.5. Embracing the Power of Positivity 34
  - 10.6. Cultivating a Growth Mindset While Balancing Well-being 34
- 11. Reflect, Adapt, Repeat: Taking Growth Into Your Own Hands 36
  - 11.1. Reflect and Revisit Your Strategies 36
  - 11.2. Adapt: Harnessing Change and Transformation 37
  - 11.3. Repeat: Committing to Continuity 37
  - 11.4. Balancing Reflection, Adaptation, and Recurrence 38
  - 11.5. Conclusion 38

The only way to do great work is to love what you do. If you haven't found it yet, keep looking. Don't settle.

— Steve Jobs

Chapter 1. Introduction

In this exciting Special Report "Growth Hacking Your Life: Practical Tips for Maximum Impact", we are set to take you on a transformative journey! Unlock the secrets to maximizing your potential and accelerating your personal growth. These practical strategies and insightful tips are not confined to any particular facet of your life. Instead, they span across your career, relationships, self-improvement, and everyday routines. This dynamic guide is fun, friendly, and packed with actionable information that promises to alter your life vividly and productively. Get ready to power through barriers, smash your goals, and land yourself in the extraordinary league. After reading this intro, if your heart feels a rush of positivity and an urge to reach out and grab life by the horns, then this Special Report is precisely what you need. Let's embark on making a more productive, happier, and fulfilling life. Dive in, elevate your life, and reach new peaks!

Chapter 2. Understanding the Growth Hacking Mindset

Growth hacking is a mindset—an outlook that champions constant learning, adaptation, and exponential growth. Fusing aspects of marketing, psychology, and data analysis, growth hacking is a potent tool leveraged by startups to foster prolific growth. However, this effective strategy is not locked to businesses; personal lives too can enjoy the benefits of the growth hacking mindset. Bountiful rewards await those willing to fidget with conventional strategies, identify potential areas for growth, and experiment relentlessly.

2.1. Sub Chapter Heading: The Importance of Developing a Growth Hacking Mindset

Cultivating a growth hacking mindset can be a pivotal step towards embarking on a productive and fulfilling life journey. This mindset encourages us to perpetually seek opportunities for improvement, resulting in consistent enhancement in personal and professional life areas. Having a growth mindset encourages self-awareness, boosts resilience, strengthens relationships, and sparks continual learning—all of which are fundamental cornerstones of self-realization and success.

2.2. Sub Chapter Heading: Recognizing Growth Opportunities

Launching into the mindset of a growth hacker, your life becomes a fertile ground, proliferating with possibilities for growth. Every hurdle is regarded as a puzzle to be solved, an opportunity for learning and improvement. Seeking out such opportunities requires a deliberate shift from the norm, embracing challenges and going against the grain. Having a lucid understanding of your strengths and weaknesses enables you to unlock your hidden potential and smash through personal or professional plateaus to propel higher.

2.3. Sub Chapter Heading: Embracing Failure as Part of the Process

As you begin to recognize growth opportunities and act upon them, it's crucial to perceive failures as stepping stones. The route to growth seldom runs smooth; there may be setbacks, obstacles, and outright failures. Acknowledging failure as an integral part of the process, rather than mere hindrances, can catalyze learning and initiate transformative growth. These painful yet indispensable experiences often offer the most valuable insights and learning opportunities.

2.4. Sub Chapter Heading: Adopting a Data-Driven Approach

Effective growth hacking strategies are usually rooted in data. A clear appreciation of your progress, behaviors, and patterns over time allows for informed decision-making and accuracy in personal growth endeavors. Recording, analyzing, and iterating on your progress will equip you with the tools you need to navigate future growth initiatives successfully. Adopting this data-driven approach fosters resilience, enabling you to quickly rebound from setbacks and adjust course when needed.

2.5. Sub Chapter Heading: Constant Experimentation and Iteration

In the realm of a growth hacker, the modus operandi is to pick an area of growth, conceive hypotheses, and implement experiments to test these hypotheses—the results of which will inform the need for pivots, optimizations, or complete overhauls. Applying this approach to personal life empowers you to insightfully experiment with different strategies, assess their efficacy, and make data-informed conclusions regarding what works best for you.

2.6. Sub Chapter Heading: Cultivating Agility

A growth hacking mindset calls for agility—the flexibility to adapt and respond effectively to changes or unforeseen circumstances. It's about staying poised in the face of adversity and turning challenges into growth opportunities. Cultivating agility entails fostering an open mindset, one ready to question existing norms and nimble enough to switch tactics when necessary.

2.7. Sub Chapter Heading: Harnessing the Power of Collaboration

Growth hacking is never a solitary endeavor, whether in business or personal life. Harnessing the collective wisdom of a community can accelerate your growth exponentially. Encouraging collaborative efforts can broaden your perspective, open doors to new ideas, and unlock unforeseen opportunities. It's about building a support network that constantly challenges and inspires you to grow.

Understanding and adopting a growth hacking mindset will set the stage for meaningful and sustainable personal growth. Join us in the next chapter as we take this new approach and start defining clear, actionable goals to kickstart your exciting journey of growth. Remember, growth isn't comfortable. But, as they say, nothing worthwhile ever is! Enjoy the journey, relish the challenging yet rewarding process, and remember - the beauty lies in the journey, not only the destination.

Chapter 3. Setting the Stage: Defining Your Goals

To begin the process of growth hacking your life, it is utterly crucial to take a deep breath, clear your mind and meticulously set your goals. This inherently strategic process is the cornerstone of your growth hacking journey.

3.1. The Importance of Goals

The pivotal role that goals play in shaping our lives cannot be overstated. Goals are beacons that guide us through the murky and often turbulent waters of life. They may appear in various shapes or forms - professional aspirations, personal ambitions, short-term undertakings or long-term dreams. Still, they all serve the purpose of defining our direction, motivating us to push beyond our limits and framing a sense of purpose in our lives.

Moreover, the S.M.A.R.T. acronym redefines goal setting effectively and provides a comprehensive framework. It stands for Specific, Measurable, Achievable, Relevant, and Time-bound. By using this framework, your goals will not only be more tangible but also easier to follow and ultimately, accomplish.

3.2. Setting S.M.A.R.T Goals

We must start by establishing **Specific** goals. It isn't beneficial merely to have vague thoughts such as, 'I want to be successful', or 'I wish to be happier'. We need to drill down into the exact details. For instance, a more specific goal might be 'I want to become a team leader in my company within the next two years' or 'I will run a half marathon six months from now'.

After making the goals specific, the next step is to ensure that they are **Measurable**. Establish tangible criteria to measure progress towards the attainment of each goal. The measurement provides a clear way of tracking the progress and makes the goal seem more real. For instance, if your goal is to read more books, set a measurable target, such as 'I will read one book per week'.

Once the goals have a measurable benchmark, establish if they are **Achievable**. Nothing can deter the spirit more than setting unachievable, outlandish goals. When setting a goal, ask yourself, 'Is this realistically achievable for me'? This does not mean that the goals have to be too easy. They should still challenge and require an effort to achieve.

Fourth, goals must be **Relevant**. They need to align with your overall vision for life and significant areas such as career, finance, health, relationships, personal development, and recreation. Consider how these goals fit into your broader life scheme and whether they propel you toward ultimate life objectives.

Finally, make the goals **Time-bound**. There must be a deadline for achieving them. A timeframe creates a sense of urgency, acting as a catalyst. It propels you forward, motivating you to push beyond your comfort zone.

3.3. The Power of Visualization

An often-underutilized tool in setting and achieving goals is visualization. Science has consistently proven that the mind cannot distinguish between reality and vividly imagined scenarios. Hence, the practice of creating a rich, vibrant mental image of you achieving your goal can have profound effects. Imagine the triumphant feeling, the surroundings, the sounds and even the smells when you finally hit your goal. Make it as detailed and tangible as possible. Visualization can indeed serve as a potent motivation propeller.

3.4. Creating A Goal Map

You've comprehensively defined your goals, inspected them through the S.M.A.R.T lens, and harnessed visualization's power. The final piece of this chapter involves mapping out your goals. A goal map is a visual or written plan delineating similarly themed goals, their respective action steps, and the resources required to achieve them.

Write down your defined goals, mark the deadline next to each. Further, break each down into smaller, manageable tasks. Define the resources you need for each task and track your progress. This goal map serves as your personal success blueprint, your roadmap towards self-growth.

3.5. In Conclusion

Setting goals is not about the frenetic rush of creating an endless to-do list. It's an intentional process of self-discovery, defining where we want to go, and deciding the best way to get there. Through clear, measurable, achievable, relevant, and time-bound goals, you can create a life course of vital impact and thriving growth. Using tools like visualization and goal mapping, you can fuel your journey to transformation and personal development. The stage is indeed set. Now, it is time to step into the spotlight and execute. Who's ready to start growth hacking their lives? Onwards and upwards we go.

On your mark, get set, grow!

Chapter 4. Mental Strategies for Persistent Progress

Our journey delves into the realm of cognition where we shed light on the varied mental strategies that are fundamental for persistent progress. These refer to the assortment of heuristics, perspectives, and mindsets that encourage continuity, resilience, and personal growth in our pursuits.

4.1. Cultivating a Growth Mindset

At the core of any strategy that promotes progress, it's paramount to foster what psychologist Carol Dweck calls a 'Growth Mindset'. Someone with a growth mindset believes their abilities, intelligence, and talent can be developed with time and effort. They perceive challenges as exciting learning opportunities and view mistakes as integral steps towards understanding and mastery.

Building a growth mindset isn't an instant process, but a journey of habitual enhancement. Start with the belief that fundamental abilities can be improved, even to a substantial degree, with perseverance, resilience, and the right strategies. Frame your environment to celebrate effort, strategies, and improvement more than the end result.

4.2. The Power of Visualization

Next, we explore the fascinating science-backed technique of mental imagery or visualization. This process involves systematically using your imagination to shape positive mental images of the desired outcomes or behaviors. Athletes, performers, and the likes often employ this strategy to prime their minds for success ahead of crucial events.

To harness visualization, identify your goals, sit in a meditative state, and create vibrant, detailed mental scenes of accomplishing these goals. Incorporate all sensory details–smell, touch, taste, sound, sight. Engage your brain's neural network to behaviorally rehearse a performance and forge the conviction that achieving your aim is not just possible, but almost inevitable.

4.3. Resilience: Bouncing Back from Adversity

Resilience is the capacity to recover quickly from difficulties, staying buoyant in the face of adversity, and treating failure not as proof of incompetence but as a crucial stepping-stone towards success. Building resilience depends on a number of factors, including positive relationships, mental agility, and self-belief.

Develop resilience by practicing self-compassion, maintaining an optimistic outlook, and adopting a problem-solving stance towards setbacks. Reach out to trusted loved ones when feeling down, and take care of your physical health - because a healthy body can be a vital reservoir of mental strength.

4.4. Mindfulness and Focus

Mindfulness is a state of open awareness where you are fully tuned into the present moment, without any judgment or distraction. It cultivates focus, alleviates stress and fosters mental tranquility, essential components of enduring progress.

To practice mindfulness, begin with a few minutes of meditative exercises each day, gradually increasing the duration. Remain in the present moment, acknowledge any thoughts that might arise without any bias or interaction, and then lightly draw your attention back to the watchful state.

4.5. Embracing an Iterative Mindset

In the final part of this chapter, we uncover the concept of an Iterative Mindset. Just like in software development, where complex systems are built through cycles of planning, execution, testing and improving, our personal growth can also benefit from an iterative approach.

To cultivate an iterative mindset, perceive your activities as experiments rather than final products. Set an aim, take action, gather feedback, learn, modify, and redo. By embracing failure and correction, you steer clear of perfectionist paralysis, gaining wisdom, versatility, and grit for the long run.

This journey through the lanes of our mind reveals that our mindset, our mental tools and strategies, are as crucial, if not more, to achieving lasting progress and personal growth. Through the cultivation of growth mindset, visualization, resilience, mindfulness, and an iterative mindset, we acquire the mental resilience and dynamism to persistently and positively move forward, irrespective of the hurdles we encounter along the way. With these strategies in our personal toolkit, we become the masters of our growth, enabling us to navigate through a flourishing life filled with learning, positivity, and accomplishment.

Chapter 5. Healthy Habits: The Foundation of Personal Growth

Harnessing the immense potential within every individual invariably begins with a focus on health, the foundation stone of personal growth. The tenet that 'Health is Wealth' encapsulates this truth beautifully. A healthy mind and body are prerequisites to fully unleash your potential; they enable you to strive towards your goals tirelessly, persevere through hurdles, and embrace growth more holistically.

5.1. The Catalysts of Health

Holistic health revolves around three critical pillars - physical wellness, mental well-being, and proper nutrition. Let's explore each of these facets individually:

5.1.1. Physical Wellness

Physical wellness implies maintaining a strong, healthy body to sustain the performance demand of our daily lives. Establishing a routine that includes regular exercise is pivotal in this endeavor. It's not necessary to plunge headfirst into strenuous workouts. Start small. You might consider walking for 30 minutes a day, then slowly escalating your efforts to jogging, and finally running. Your exercise routine can be anything from yoga, swimming, cycling, to weight training, as long as it gets your body moving. Regular physical activity ensures fitness, builds immunity, and increases energy levels. Furthermore, it stimulates the production of endorphins, the body's natural painkillers and mood elevators, promoting overall mental well-being.

5.1.2. Mental Well-being

In today's fast-paced world, mental health often takes a backseat. However, it's as crucial as physical health. Mindfulness practices like meditation, deep breathing exercises, or simply cultivating an awareness of your surroundings contribute significantly towards mental health by reducing stress, boosting memory, and improving focus. Emphasizing adequate sleep is another essential aspect of maintaining our brains' health. Restful sleep acts as a reset button; it boosts your mood, reenergizes your body, and powers your cognitive functions.

5.1.3. Proper Nutrition

The phrase 'you are what you eat' underscores the impact of our dietary choices on our overall health. Consuming a balanced diet rich in fresh fruits, vegetables, lean proteins, whole grains, and healthy fats fuels your body and mind, enhancing productivity and reducing susceptibility to diseases. Minimizing your sugar and processed food intake while adequately hydrating can radically improve your overall health and vitality.

5.2. Embodying Healthy Habits

Once we understand the fundamental components of health, the next step is to embody these healthy habits fully. These are a few strategies that can help:

5.2.1. Habit Stacking

Developing a new behavior can be challenging. To simplify, leverage the concept of 'habit stacking.' This strategy involves adding your new habit to an existing routine. For instance, if you aim to meditate daily, pair it with a current habit, perhaps right after brushing your teeth in the morning or before hitting the bed at night.

5.2.2. Progress Over Perfection

Perfectionism can be debilitating. Instead, embrace a mindset of progress over perfection. Applaud your small wins of the day, such as choosing a healthy snack over a sugary one. These small victories accumulate over time, contributing to substantial growth.

5.2.3. Accountability

To make your new habits stick, consider having an accountability partner. Sharing your goals with a trusted person who checks on your progress can dramatically increase your success likelihood.

5.3. The Ripple Effect

When integrated diligently, healthy habits set off a positive chain reaction beyond physical and mental benefits. They instill discipline and resilience, qualities necessary for personal growth.

In conclusion, the practice of leading a healthy lifestyle intertwines with your overall personal growth journey. By incorporating healthy habits into our daily routines, we not just facilitate our physical and mental well-being but ultimately create meaningful, lasting changes towards becoming the best versions of ourselves. Remember, the path of personal growth begins with a series of small, focused steps leading towards larger objectives. Start today, and you'll soon witness the undisputed impact these habits have on shaping and enhancing the trajectory of your growth.

Chapter 6. Career Advancement Techniques: Hack Your Way Up

Starting straight away, let's probe into the multifaceted world of accelerating your career. You are not merely a passenger on this journey; you are in the driver's seat, equipped with the potential to steer your career in any direction you choose using growth hacking techniques.

6.1. Encouraging a Growth Mindset

Firstly, it's crucial to incubate a growth mindset, a concept propounded by psychologist Carol Dweck. A growth mindset promotes the belief that you and your ability to succeed are not static. You have the capacity to learn, adapt, and improve. Your skills, both hard and soft, can be honed with committed practice, and challenges can be overcome through resilience and persistence.

Pertaining intentionally to career advancement, this concept signifies that no job or role is beyond your reach if you're ready to learn and invest in self-improvement. Be audacious in setting your career goals, and let the growth mindset help you achieve them.

6.2. Mastering Your Current Role

By virtuously mastering your existing role, you plan a foundation for onward movement. Take note of each job task you perform and strive to become exceedingly proficient at them. Which tasks were challenging? Which tasks were stimulating? What components of your role yield the most significant results and give you the most satisfaction? These insights provide a roadmap of areas where you can improve.

Going the extra mile, taking initiatives, showing consistency, and delivering top-quality work makes you invaluable in your role and sets the platform for advancement. Proposing and implementing ideas for improvement and solving complex problems can set you apart.

6.3. Building Influential Relationships

Every organization, regardless of its size, operates as a nexus of relationships. To forge your path up the career ladder, it's indispensable to develop excellent networking skills. Relationships with peers, superiors, and employees in other departments can significantly influence your career development.

Make a genuine attempt to connect with colleagues, participate in meetings and gatherings, show your support for others, and express your ideas respectfully. Don't hesitate to seek advice when needed. You'll not only gain significant insights but also earn the reputation of being a team player, leading to better opportunities.

6.4. Branding Yourself

To ensure that your skills and potential are recognized, consider enhancing your personal brand. This entails representing yourself as a high-value individual that organizations aspire to retain. Your personal brand should echo your abilities, work ethics, and core values.

Cultivate your brand on various platforms, external and internal. Regularly updating your LinkedIn profile with your achievements and projects, participating in relevant forums and communities, contributing to industry discussions, and networking at professional events, all contribute to your personal brand.

6.5. Priority on Skill Building

The most successful careers are built by continuous learning and skilling. Proactively identify key skills needed in your desired role or industry, and invest time in acquiring them. Online platforms offer a plethora of courses and certifications in numerous domains.

Never underestimate soft skills; they are as vital as hard skills. Emotional intelligence, team collaboration, problem-solving, leadership abilities, and excellent communication can dramatically improve your chances of promotion.

6.6. Seeking Out and Responding to Feedback

Regular feedback - both positive and constructive criticism - is essential to understand your strengths, weaknesses, and areas needing improvement. Don't shy away from feedback; instead, seek it out. Display your ability to accept, adapt, and improve. This growth-oriented approach is highly favored and can steer your career upwards.

6.7. Be Adaptable

Finally, one of the most crucial attributes in today's fast-paced professional world is adaptability. Change is constant in every enterprise, and agility in embracing changes — like new technologies, workflows, or strategies — signifies your commitment and value to the organization.

In conclusion, these career growth hacking techniques can forge a pathway for you to climb up the corporate ladder. It's a slow and gradual process that requires perseverance, learning, interaction, adaptability, and a consistent drive towards personal and professional enhancement. Remember, the keys to your career advancement lie within your own hands. So, strap up, take charge, and drive your way to empowerment and success.

Chapter 7. Improving Relationships: Connect Deeper, Grow Together

Delving into the intricate threads of relationships, one discovers an innate power, an undeniably potent factor that immeasurably enriches the quality of life and personal fulfillment. This exclusive chapter will examine the art and science of improving relationships from the ground up, threading together essential elements like emotional intelligence, impactful communication, mutual respect, patience, understanding, and empathy along the way.

7.1. Emotional Intelligence: The Cornerstone

At the beating heart of every healthy relationship lies a core principle: emotional intelligence. It is the crux of understanding, relating to, and harnessing your emotions and those of others. Emotional intelligence shapes our narratives, actions and reactions in relationships. When you nurture your emotional intelligence, you become proficient in managing your feelings, not just identifying them. Emotional intelligence triggers self-awareness, leading to better self-regulation, empathy, and inter-personal relationships.

Elevating your emotional intelligence requires purposeful effort and practice. Endeavor to perceive your emotions without judgment. Practice assessing your feelings with patience and understanding, explore the triggers, and recognize patterns. With consistent reflection, you can improve your emotional intelligence a step at a time.

7.2. Impactful Communication: The Lifeline of Relationships

There are myriad forms of communication - from non-verbal cues transmitted silently, to vocalized emotions, to messages typed hastily into electric screens. The dynamic nature of communication makes it a significant lever in strengthening relationships. Attuned, attentive, and purposeful communication can bridge gaps, address misunderstandings, and forge bonds.

Start with active listening - a cornerstone of impactful communication. Active listening is about becoming an active participant in a conversation, offering emotional availability, confirmation, clarification, and understanding. Refrain from planning your rebuttal while the other person speaks – this reduces your ability to comprehend their viewpoint fully.

Additionally, it's imperative to express yourself and your needs clearly. Honesty and openness, tempered with empathy and respect, form the foundation for effective communication.

7.3. Mutual Respect: The Pillar of Longevity

Nothing sustains a relationship longer than mutual respect. This weighty element lends dignity, promotes trust, and strengthens bonds. Respecting another's time, perspectives, emotions, and choices fosters a safe space for growth and mutual appreciation.

Integrating respect into practice can sometimes be challenging. It requires us to acknowledge and appreciate the differences that permeate each relationship, understanding that each person brings a unique worldview to the table. Where there is respect, there is an allowance for individuality and room for character growth.

7.4. Patience, Understanding, and Empathy: The Essential Triumvirate

Imperfections tint our existence, making our life a rich tapestry of triumphs and trials, strengths and weaknesses. Patience, understanding, and empathy give life to acceptance, creating an atmosphere where people can be authentically themselves.

Patience must be cultivated, a seedling nurtured into a robust tree. It is the bedrock upon which understanding and empathy stand, allowing time and space for others to reveal themselves, their thoughts, and their feelings without fear.

Understanding comes with sincere efforts to perceive motivations, hardships, dreams, and emotions. By putting yourself in the shoes of others and contemplating their perspective, empathy is born - a resilient bridge that connects two souls in a profound way.

7.5. Building Bonds: Nurture to Flourish

Once the foundations have been laid, fostering a relationship requires consistent effort. It demands attention to the imperfections, nurturing the strengths, and honoring the uniqueness of the individuals involved.

Practicing gratitude is one such tool. It can shift perspectives, foster positivity, and enhance connection. Regularly acknowledge and appreciate the goodness the other brings into your life.

Create shared experiences together. Shared experiences strengthen bonds, create beautiful memories and develop mutual understanding. By participating in activities and adventures, you can celebrate the joys of life together.

Lastly, invest in regular, quality time with each other. Time is a precious commodity: when you consciously allot it to your relationship, it sends a potent message – that this relationship is valuable, worthy and deserving of your attention.

In closing, improving relationships encompasses a broader canvas beyond these subheadings. It's an art and a science that unifies myriad elements into a cohesive process. Remember, each relationship is unique in its complexity and simplicity, in its capacity to bring joy and challenges. As you embark on improving your relationships, may the journey be illuminative, enriching, and deeply rewarding.

Chapter 8. Mastering Time Management: More Life in Your Day

If there's a single resource that is equally distributed among all individuals, it is Time. Whether wealthy or poor, young or old, everyone on this planet is given the same 24 hours a day, making time one of the most democratic of all resources. There's no hoarding, no storing, no hitting pause, no rewinding. It's relentless. But, time is unquestionably the most valuable resource, hence the age-old saying, "Time is Gold."

So, how do you ensure that you make every minute count? As we delve into the art and science of time management, we'll explore practical techniques, practices, and insights to help you maximize productivity and enjoy more life in your everyday routine.

8.1. Understanding Time: The Commodity You Can't Store

If not properly managed, time has a way of slipping away from us. You may have observed days when time seems to fly, and hours vanish into thin air with hardly anything accomplished. When you understand the true essence of time, you start valuing it. Honoring your obligations, appointments, and commitments begets respect from your peers, who recognize your adherence to time as a reflection of your professional and personal respect for them. It's also important not to mistake being busy for being productive. Therefore, comprehension of the dynamic nature of time is vital for realizing its true value.

8.2. Keys of Time Management

Time management is one of the effective measures to hack your life and trigger growth—but what does efficient time management comprise? It's essentially grounded in planning and organizing time between specific activities to increase productivity and efficiency. Here, we'll discuss the core principles or keys of time management: Prioritization, Delegation, Goal-setting and Following a routine.

1. Prioritization: Honing your ability to prioritize tasks according to their urgency and importance is crucial. Using the Eisenhower Box, a powerful tool for prioritizing and decision-making, is extremely beneficial in this area.
2. Delegation: Not every task requires direct involvement. Understanding when to delegate and to whom can save considerable time that can be utilized for other significant tasks.
3. Goal-setting: When you work without a clear goal or end-point in mind, it's similar to sailing without a destination. It helps if you set SMART (Specific, Measurable, Achievable, Relevant and Time-bound) goals.
4. Following a routine: A well-structured routine brings discipline and saves the mental effort of decision-making about what to do next.

8.3. Time Management Techniques

A myriad of time management techniques are available, and different techniques work for different individuals. Here are some popular and effective approaches:

1. Pomodoro Technique: It breaks your work into specific time intervals, typically 25 minutes, followed by a 5-minute break. This method promotes focus and helps maintain your mental agility.

2. Time blocking: This involves allocating specific, pre-planned time slots to different tasks.

3. The Eisenhower Matrix: Helps to distinguish urgent and important tasks, those that can be scheduled for later, and tasks to delegate or eliminate.

4. The 80/20 Rule, or Pareto Principle: Implies that 80% of your outcomes come from 20% of your inputs. Identifying and focusing on these high-impact activities can maximize productivity.

8.4. Time Management Tools

To augment the effect of time management techniques, plenty of time management tools are available today. Digital tools like calendars, task management apps, and productivity suites can aid in efficiently managing and allocating your time.

8.5. The Outcome of Effective Time Management

Exceptional time management can yield considerable benefits, such as:

1. Enhanced productivity and efficiency.
2. An increased sense of control and competency.
3. Improved work-life balance.
4. Reduced stress and anxiety.
5. Opportunities for growth and learning.

8.6. Reassessing and Refining Your Time Management Strategy

The path to effective time management is typically iterative and demands consistent reassessment. What works for one person might not work as effectively for another, and what works for you today might not work as efficiently tomorrow. Regularly assessing and refining your time management strategy is indispensable.

Bear in mind the keys to time management and the techniques involved, deploy digital tools to work smarter, not harder, reap the benefits, and continuously refine your tactics to get more life into your day. Once you master time, you master life.

By adopting the best practices of time management, you gain the ability to dictate the pace of your life. Remember, the clock is ticking, and every moment wasted can never be reclaimed. Invest your time wisely to yield a life of fulfillment, success, and happiness.

Chapter 9. Continuous Learning: The Key to Unlimited Growth

Let's commence our journey into the illuminating realm of continuous learning, where we postulate the fundamental idea that growth, in its unending capacities, stems from an insatiable thirst for knowledge. This chapter promises to initiate a profound transformation, transforming ordinary individuals into growth hackers by developing their continuous learning techniques. Filled with insightful information and actionable guidance, we will delve deep into the sea of knowledge absorption, showing you how learning can become your passport to unlimited personal growth and a fulfilled life.

9.1. Embracing the Learning Mindset

First and foremost, we need to acknowledge and embrace the learning mindset. This is the intrinsic belief that you can always develop and expand your capabilities. Perhaps one of the physics' greatest minds, Albert Einstein, beautifully encapsulated this idea when he said: "Once you stop learning, you start dying". Hence, stepping into a mental zone where you view yourself as an ever-evolving learner and are open to new concepts and ideas, even when they challenge your existing worldviews, is the key to unlimited personal growth.

One technique to embrace the learning mindset is the practice of growth mindset, coined by psychologist Carol Dweck. According to Dweck, those with a growth mindset believe they can develop their abilities through strategy, effort, and approaching challenges wholeheartedly. Meanwhile, individuals with a fixed mindset tend to believe their talents are inherent, hence barring them from their growth potential. Adapting a growth mindset can make the difference in how we approach learning and reclaim control over our growth trajectory.

9.2. Learning Modalities: Discover the Way That Fits You

The next step in integrating continuous learning in our life is identifying our preferred learning styles or modalities. Although the appeal and effectiveness of learning styles have been challenged recently, understanding your preferred modality can optimize the learning process. Howard Gardner's Theory of Multiple Intelligences outlines several modalities such as visual-spatial, auditory-musical, logical-mathematical, interpersonal, intrapersonal, bodily-kinesthetic, linguistic, and naturalistic.

A majority of learners are categorized as multimodal, meaning they learn best using a combination of learning styles. For example, auditory learners absorb information quickly through listening, while visual learners benefit greatly from diagrams, charts, or other visual aids. By understanding your personal style, you can tailor your learning experiences to best suit your unique strengths.

9.3. Find Your Learning Sources

While it's pivotal to have the thirst for knowledge, it's equally essential to know where to quench it. Fortunately, we live in the era of information where knowledge is ubiquitous and readily available. Ranging from online courses on platforms like Coursera or Udemy, podcasts ranging from science to self-improvement, books on every topic imaginable, mentorship programs, workshops, or even social media platforms with educational content, the options are endless.

However, having numerous sources can also lead to information overload. To counter this, one must learn to discern and choose the most reliable and relevant sources. Formulating a learning plan, systematically outlining what we want to learn, when we want to learn, and from where, prevents us from drowning in a sea of excessive information.

9.4. Building Consistent Learning Routines

Understanding and appreciating the value of learning is not enough — one must translate this comprehension into concrete action. Incorporating learning into your daily micro-routines can guarantee consistent progress. Whether it's reading a chapter of a book before sleep or listening to a podcast during your commute, efficient planning can blend learning seamlessly into your everyday life.

Creating a dedicated learning space at home, be it a reading nook or a home office, can provide an ambiance conducive to knowledge absorption. Try different approaches: digital detox hours for distraction-free reading, learning partnerships for accountability, or morning learning routines to kickstart your day —find what works best for you.

9.5. Curating and Implementing the Learned Knowledge

Lastly, the continuous learning process reaches fruition when we apply what we have learned. Skills stagnate if not put into practice. Furthermore, share and discuss what you've learned with others. Teaching is not only a fantastic way to reinforce your understanding but also contributes to the community of learners and promotes collective growth.

It's also highly beneficial to maintain a learning journal. This record not only monitors your progress but also serves as a space for reflection. It helps consolidate your knowledge but also provides insight into your learning methods and identifies possible avenues for improvement.

To put succinctly, continuous learning unleashes the boundless potential that lies within each one of us. With the right mindset, the understanding of our unique learning styles, discernment in choosing our learning sources, and the translation of knowledge into everyday practice, we can attain untrammeled growth. Remember, learning is not a task to be completed, but a journey to be enjoyed, one that leads to the undying essence of personal advancement, empowerment, and fulfilment.

Chapter 10. Maintaining Balance: Managing Growth Without Burnout

Despite the exhilarating journey towards growth, it's essential to incorporate balance to ensure that the flame of your ever-growing potential doesn't burn out. This chapter addresses the critical aspect of maintaining balance while persistently seeking growth. We delve into strategies, techniques, and initiatives that can help manage advancements without letting them overwhelm your life and making your journey toward self-improvement a gratifying, sustainable endeavor rather than a draining struggle.

10.1. Understanding the Importance of Balance

Imagine growth as a high-speed train. When it's running on track, it takes you towards wonderful destinations. However, if you continually keep speeding it up without allowing for necessary breaks, not only does the journey become uncomfortable and exhausting, but there's a probable risk of derailment. As such, balance is the equivalent of implementing strategic breaks and speed management in your growth journey. It's a way of fine-tuning your path, allowing you to enjoy, reflect, and refresh amid pursuing your goals. It's about knowing when to push and when to pause.

10.2. Recognizing the Symptoms of Burnout

Burnout is a common byproduct of unchecked growth. It's characterized by mental, emotional, and physical exhaustion, and is often associated with increased disengagement, decreased productivity, and deteriorated mental health. Key symptoms include chronic fatigue, insomnia, frequent forgetfulness, increased illness, anxiety, depression, anger, loss of appetite, diminished concentration, and a general sense of disillusionment or cynicism. If you recognize many of these symptoms, it may be a hint that you're burning the growth candle at both ends and need to foster better balance.

10.3. Building Balance into Your Growth Plan

To prevent burnout and ensure a sustainable journey toward your goals, it's paramount to integrate balance into your growth plan. Start by scheduling downtime and breaks into your daily routine, ensuring that there's always an uninterrupted time for relaxation and rejuvenation. Engage in activities that help you unwind, indulge in hobbies, or simply have periods of stillness and reflection. This inclusion supports mental clarity, bolsters emotional stability, and decreases stress levels.

Further, maintain healthy boundaries around your work commitments. Even though growth often requires an extra push, remember that overwork is counterproductive and leads to diminished performance over time. Strive to have clear delineations between your work time, personal time, and time for growth pursuits.

It's also valuable to add physical exercise into your balance plan. Physical activity has profound effects on mental health, including reducing symptoms of anxiety and depression, improving mood, and triggering the release of endorphins, the body's natural mood boosters. Moreover, physical activity can enhance cognitive function, leading to improved focus and better performance in your growth pursuits.

10.4. Mastering the Art of Stress Management

Stress management is another crucial aspect of maintaining balance. Although stress can sometimes be beneficial, acting as a motivator and a catalyst for growth, chronic unmanaged stress is detrimental. Techniques such as relaxation exercises, mindfulness meditation, deep breathing, and yoga can help in reducing stress levels. Additionally, maintaining a nutritious diet, ensuring adequate sleep, and having a solid support circle of friends and family are noted ways to help manage stress.

10.5. Embracing the Power of Positivity

Maintaining a positive mindset is another integral part of achieving balance. Positivity fuels resilience and empowers you to handle difficulties more effectively. Indulge in affirmations, surround yourself with positive company, journal your achievements and moments of gratitude, cultivate humor and try to see the bigger picture during challenging times. Remember, growth is not merely about reaching milestones but equally about the journey and the person you become along the way.

10.6. Cultivating a Growth Mindset While Balancing Well-being

Finally, coupling a balanced lifestyle with a growth mindset is key. Embrace failures and challenges as opportunities for learning. Learn to receive feedback, maintain a sense of curiosity, and practise the discipline of reflection. Without sacrificing your well-being, continue aiming for improvement, persist in the face of setbacks, and develop your skills and abilities. By integrating a balanced lifestyle and a growth mindset, the voyage becomes genuinely gratifying.

Maintaining balance is truly a multifaceted endeavor, requiring constant diligence. But, by successfully managing it, you are not just preventing burnout or merely surviving; instead, you are thriving. You are building a sturdy foundation that allows you to enjoy the process, consistently grow, and ultimately, unlock your limitless potential. Remember, balance is not about shambling along but indeed about mastering the art of living, growing, and thriving sustainively.

Chapter 11. Reflect, Adapt, Repeat: Taking Growth Into Your Own Hands

As we draw near to the culmination of our growth hacking guide, it's time to concentrate on the paramount importance of reflection, adaptation, and repetition in the process of personal advancement. This holistic approach merges the aspects we have learned so far, leading us towards a system of constant growth and learning. The essence here lies not only in the implementation of the strategies but also in continuously observing their effects, adapting to the insights gained, and repeating the process to evolve continually. This cyclical process is integral to realizing our aspirations and is the foundation of continuous self-improvement.

11.1. Reflect and Revisit Your Strategies

To begin with, reflecting on our actions is crucial. Each strategy you implement comes with its dataset of experiences, outcomes, and insights. Reflecting on these aspects helps us intricately understand our journey, decipher our strengths, discern our weaknesses, and revise our strategies with newfound intelligence. Systematically pausing to deliberate upon our choices, actions, and ensuing results helps maintain perspective and encourages meaningful growth.

Reflection comes in many forms. You might opt for a quiet contemplation at the end of the day, assessing the events that unfolded and how they affected you. This could involve delving into how you reacted, responded, or failed to respond in certain situations. Journaling your thoughts, feelings, and experiences can be another beneficial practice. It offers you a tangible record of your journey from which patterns and insights can be drawn.

Furthermore, feedback—both external and self-generated—acts as another potent source for reflection. Consider regular check-ins with people you trust, who can provide an external perspective on your growth progress, or use personal self-checkpoint systems to evaluate your progress objectively. Inviting feedback and critiques, and implementing reflections, are consequential aspects of growth hacking our lives.

11.2. Adapt: Harnessing Change and Transformation

Once you have reflected upon your efforts and discerned the patterns, it's time to adapt. Adaptation is the key to survival and progress. In this context, it involves fine-tuning your strategies and approaches based on the insights you have gathered from reflection.

Adapting could mean altering your approach towards a particular goal if the current one isn't serving you well. It could mean calibrating your mindset, discarding negative paradigms, and adopting more positive ones. It could also involve recognizing that a certain goal no longer serves your ultimate purpose, allowing you to divert your energies more productively. Adaptation takes courage, acceptance, and flexibility—the courage to face the results constructively; acceptance of the shortcomings, failures, or changes needed; and the flexibility to alter course as necessary.

11.3. Repeat: Committing to Continuity

After reflection and adaptation, comes the final yet everlasting step: repetition. Continuous personal growth requires investment in an unending cycle of reflection and adaptation. As we evolve, our journey of growth doesn't have an endpoint—it's a lifelong journey that renews with each passing phase of life.

By waiving the notion of a final destination, we embrace the process as the primary source of personal growth. When dedicated to repeating the cycle—reflect, adapt, repeat—we free ourselves from the constraints and pressures of striving for perfection. Instead, we create an environment of perpetual growth and transformation that brings its rewards.

11.4. Balancing Reflection, Adaptation, and Recurrence

While pursuing the reflect-adapt-repeat cycle, remember to maintain a balance. Over-reflection can lead to stagnation or overthinking, hampering progress. Similarly, adaptation should not lead to constant course-changing causing instability. Repetition is beneficial when it signifies commitment to growth, not rigid monotony. Striking balance in these aspects accelerates growth while ensuring sustainability of progress.

By maintaining this cycle, we participate actively in our growth journey. Moreover, it allows for the evolution of our growth hacking mindset, multiplying the impact and augmenting our lives multi-dimensionally.

11.5. Conclusion

Through this chapter, a recurring theme is evident: growth hacking isn't a one-and-done process—it's an endless cycle of forward movement, reflection, adaptation, and renewal. The willingness to enter this cyclical process and commit to the growth journey makes the pathway clearer, as it constantly offers opportunities for meaningful change and transformation. Consistency in these practices will lead to a rewarding, balanced life, rich in growth and learning.

The power of growth hacking lies fundamentally in our hands—through our choices, actions, reactions, and commitment to reflection, adaptation, and relentless progress. In closing, remember this key mantra: reflect, adapt, repeat. Retain it, respect it, and revisit it throughout your growth journey. This could be your powerful catalyst toward a productive, satisfying, and fulfilling life—one that is always in the making, continuously evolving, and endlessly rewarding!

www.ingramcontent.com/pod-product-compliance
Lightning Source LLC
Chambersburg PA
CBHW070953220526
45471CB00007B/3006